THE POWER OF POSITIVE HABITS

BUILDING YOUR LIFE ON A FOUNDATION OF SUCCESS

DR. JAGADEESH PILLAI

|| Dedicated to all wisdom seekers around the World ||

ॐ

Contents

Contents

Prayer

"Om Bhadram Karnebhih Shrunuyaama DevaahBhadram Pashyemaakshabhiryajatraah SthirairangaistushtuvaamsastanoobhihVyashema Devahitam YadaayuhSwasti Na Indro VridhashravaahSwasti Nah Pooshaa VishwavedaahSwasti Nastaarkshyo ArishtanemihSwasti No Brihaspatir DadhaatuOm Shantih, Shantih, Shantih"

The literal meaning of this mantra is: OM. O Gods! Let us hear auspicious words from our ears. O reverent Gods! Let us behold propitious visions from our eyes, let our organs and body be stable, healthy, and strong. Let us do that which is pleasing to the gods in the life span allotted to us. May Indra, inscribed in the scriptures, bring us fortune! May Pushan, the knower of the world, grant us prosperity! May Trakshya, who vanquishes enemies, bestow us with blessings! May Brihaspati bring us success!
OM Peace, Peace, Peace.

About The Author

Dr. Jagadeesh Pillai is a renowned Guinness World Record holder, writer, and researcher hailing from Varanasi, also known as the abode of Lord Shiva. With a Ph.D. in Vedic Science and a range of creative ideas and achievements, he is a true polymath. He is the author of more than 100 books including Research Publications. Although his roots can be traced back to Kerala, the people of Varanasi hold him in high regard and affectionately consider him one of their own.

In 1998, Dr. Pillai was offered a job at Banaras Hindu University, but he left the position after only two months to pursue greater goals in life. He believed that in order to study Indian scriptures and engage in other creative endeavours, he needed to retire from the daily grind of working solely for money at a young age.

He started an export business from scratch, using the knowledge he had gained from a previous job in the industry. His intelligence and unique approach to business led to great success in a short period of time, earning him more in just a decade and a half than he would have in a lifetime working in a government job. Upon the passing of Dr. APJ Abdul Kalam, Dr. Pillai decided to leave the business and dedicate himself to reading, studying, researching, and experimenting.

During his tenure in the export business, Dr. Pillai traveled to over 16 countries, gaining valuable insight and experiencing the world and life in detail.

Dr. Pillai has achieved four Guinness World Records in the following subjects:

"Script to Screen" - In this record, Dr. Pillai produced and directed an animation film within the shortest time possible, breaking the previous record set by Canadians. He has also received numerous national and international awards and recognitions for this achievement.

Longest Line of Postcards - For this record, Dr. Pillai created a line of 16,300 postcards on the occasion of the 163rd anniversary of Indian Postal Day. The event also included a questionnaire about the Indian flag.

Largest Poster Awareness Campaign - Dr. Pillai designed an awareness campaign on the subject of "Beti Bachao - Beti Padhao" (Save the Girl Child - Educate the Girl Child) to achieve this record.

Largest Envelope - In tribute to the Indian Prime Minister's "Make in India" initiative, Dr. Pillai created a 4000 square meter envelope using waste paper to achieve this record.

Attempted - **70000 Candles on a 210 kg Cake** - To celebrate the 70th Indian Independence Day, Dr. Pillai attempted to light 70,000 candles on a 210 kg cake, which was recorded in World Records India.

Attempted - **Documentary on Dhamek Stupa of Sarnath in 17 Languages** - Dr. Pillai attempted to create a documentary on the Dhamek Stupa of Sarnath, dubbing it in 17 different languages. The result of this attempt is currently awaiting confirmation from the Guinness World Records.

Dr. Pillai is skilled in teaching the Bhagavad Gita, a Hindu scripture, and is popular among young people. He has helped many young people improve their lives through his motivational teachings.

In addition to teaching, he has composed and sung numerous Sanskrit Bhajans and patriotic songs.

He has also written and directed several short films and documentaries for awareness campaigns, and has volunteered with the police in both UP and Kerala to spread awareness about various issues through videos and photography.

Incredibly, he has produced and directed over 100 documentaries about the city of Varanasi, all on his own.

He has also helped and guided more than 25 boys and girls to achieve world records through creative and innovative methods. He is a multifaceted person who uses his intellect and the blessings given to him by God to excel in various areas. He is both a teacher and a student, always learning and teaching, and is able to master any subject he comes across.

He is a selfless social activist and motivational speaker who has overcome struggles and failures to become a successful and enthusiastic individual with a rich life experience.

In addition to his work with the Bhagavad Gita, he is also an efficient Tarot card reader, Astro-Vastu consultant, and a talented singer and composer. He has sung the entire Ram Charita Manas and Bhagavad Gita in his own compositions, and has sung the phrase "Lokah Samastha Sukhino Bhavantu" in 50 different languages. He is currently working on a detailed and scientific study of Vedas, Upanishads, Puranas, and the Bhagavad Gita. He has also composed and sung the Hanuman Chalisa and Gayatri Mantra in 108 and 1008 different compositions, respectively.

Awards - Four Times Guinness World Records, Winner of Mahatma Gandhi Vishwa Shanti Puraskar, Mahatma Gandhi Global Peace Ambassador, Kashi Ratna Award, Dr. APJ Abdul Kalam Motivational Person of the Year 2017, Mother Teresa Award, Indira Gandhi Priyadarshini Award, Bharat Vikas Ratna Award, Udyog Ratna Award, Vigyan Prasar Award, Poorvanchal Ratn Samman.

Preface

Habits have a profound impact on our lives, shaping who we are and what we achieve. They can either work for us or against us, pushing us towards our goals or holding us back. This book is dedicated to exploring the power of positive habits and how they can be harnessed to build a life of success and happiness.

Throughout the pages of this book, you will learn about the science behind habits, how to set achievable goals and create a positive habit plan, the importance of self-care and resilience, the role of positive thinking and gratitude, and much more. By the end of this book, you will have a deep understanding of the importance of positive habits and the tools you need to build them into your daily life.We hope that this book inspires and empowers you to take control of your habits and build a life of success on a foundation of positivity and happiness. So, let's get started!

I

Understanding the Power of Positive Habits and Their Impact on Success

Habits are a powerful force in our lives, shaping our daily routines and determining our level of success. Positive habits, in particular, can have a profound impact on our lives, leading to greater happiness, success, and fulfillment. In this chapter, we will explore the concept of positive habits and the impact they can have on our lives.

Positive habits are behaviors that we engage in regularly, often without conscious thought, that lead to positive outcomes. These habits can be anything from exercise and healthy eating to reading and goal-setting. They are formed through repeated behavior and are reinforced over time, becoming automatic and almost second nature.

The importance of positive habits cannot be overstated. By regularly engaging in positive habits, we are able to develop a foundation of success that supports our efforts to achieve our goals. This foundation provides a strong platform for growth and progress, allowing us to build on our successes and overcome obstacles with greater ease.

One of the key benefits of positive habits is that they help us to develop a positive mindset. By regularly engaging in activities that make us feel good and contribute to our success, we are able to cultivate a positive outlook and approach to life. This mindset is essential for success, as it helps us to focus on our goals and keep moving forward, even when faced with challenges.

Another benefit of positive habits is that they help us to manage our time and energy more effectively. By making time for positive activities, we are able to prioritize our efforts and allocate our resources in a way that supports our goals. This allows us to be more productive and efficient, enabling us to achieve more in less time.

Positive habits also help us to develop discipline and self-control. By consistently engaging in positive behaviors, we are able to build our willpower and determination, enabling us to overcome temptations and stay focused on our goals. This self-discipline is essential for success, as it allows us to maintain our focus and momentum, even when faced with obstacles or distractions.

Yes, the power of positive habits cannot be underestimated. They provide us with a foundation of success that supports our efforts to achieve our goals, helping us to develop a positive mindset, manage our time and energy more effectively, and build discipline and self-control. By developing and reinforcing positive habits, we can build a life that is rich, fulfilling, and truly successful.

"Success is not final, failure is not fatal: it is
the courage to continue that counts."

- Winston Churchill

ℂℋ

II

Setting Goals and Creating a Positive Habit Plan

Creating a successful life starts with setting goals and taking action to achieve them. However, it can be difficult to maintain motivation and focus, especially when faced with obstacles and distractions. Positive habits provide a solution to this problem, offering a roadmap for success and helping us to turn our goals into realities. In this chapter, we will explore the process of setting goals and creating a positive habit plan, and how this can help you build your life on a foundation of success.

Setting Goals

The first step in building a successful life is to set clear and specific goals. These goals should be aligned with your values and aspirations, and should reflect what is truly important to you. Goals can be related to any area of your life, including personal, professional, financial, or health and wellness.

When setting goals, it is important to be specific and to include deadlines for completion. This will help you to focus your efforts and to measure your progress over time. Additionally, breaking down large goals into smaller, achievable steps can make them more manageable and less daunting.

Creating a Positive Habit Plan

Once you have set your goals, the next step is to create a positive habit plan that will help you to achieve them. A positive habit plan is a roadmap for success, outlining the specific actions you will take to turn your goals into realities. This plan should include:

A clear description of the positive habit you wish to develop

The specific steps you will take to establish this habit

A schedule for when you will engage in this habit

Strategies for overcoming obstacles and maintaining your motivation

A system for tracking your progress and celebrating your successes

When developing your positive habit plan, it is important to start small and to focus on a few habits at a time. This will help you to avoid becoming overwhelmed and to ensure that you are making steady progress towards your goals. Additionally, it is important to be flexible and to adjust your plan as needed, in response to your changing circumstances and priorities.

The Benefits of Setting Goals and Creating a Positive Habit Plan

By setting goals and creating a positive habit plan, you are taking control of your life and building a foundation for success. This process helps you to:

Focus your efforts and align your actions with your values and aspirations

Establish a clear roadmap for success, outlining the steps you need to take to achieve your goals

Maintain motivation and focus, even when faced with obstacles and distractions

Track your progress and measure your success, helping you to stay motivated and on track

Celebrate your successes, building confidence and momentum towards your goals

Surely, setting goals and creating a positive habit plan is an essential step in building a successful life. This process helps you to align your actions with your values and aspirations, and provides a roadmap for success that will help you to overcome obstacles and achieve your goals with greater ease. By taking this step, you can build your life on a foundation of success and create a future filled with happiness and fulfillment.

"Believe in yourself and all that you are.
Know that there is something inside you that
is greater than any obstacle."

- Christian D. Larson

∞

III

Building a Daily Routine for Positive Habits

One of the most effective ways to establish positive habits and build a successful life is to incorporate them into your daily routine. A daily routine provides structure and consistency, helping you to make positive habits a priority and to ensure that you are taking consistent action towards your goals.

In this chapter, we will explore the steps involved in building a daily routine for positive habits, and how this can help you to achieve success and happiness in all areas of your life.

Step 1: Evaluate Your Current Daily Routine

The first step in building a daily routine for positive habits is to evaluate your current routine. This involves reflecting on your current habits, behaviors, and routines, and considering what changes you need to make in order to prioritize positive habits. Some questions to consider include:

What are your current habits and routines?

What are the habits and routines that are hindering your success and happiness?

What are the positive habits that you need to prioritize in order to achieve your goals?

Step 2: Identify Your Priorities

Once you have evaluated your current daily routine, the next step is to identify your priorities. This involves determining what is most important to you and what you need to focus on in order to achieve your goals. Some areas to consider when identifying your priorities include:

Personal growth and self-improvement

Professional development and career success

Financial stability and wealth building

Physical and mental health and wellness

Relationships and social connections

Step 3: Create a Schedule for Your Positive Habits

With your priorities in mind, the next step is to create a schedule for your positive habits. This schedule should outline the specific actions you will take each day to prioritize your positive habits and build a foundation for success. Some tips for creating a schedule for your positive habits include:

Starting each day with your most important habits

Allocating specific times for each positive habit

Incorporating breaks and free time into your schedule

Being flexible and adjusting your schedule as needed

Step 4: Make Positive Habits a Priority

Once you have created a schedule for your positive habits, the next step is to make them a priority. This involves setting aside time each day to focus on your positive habits and to ensure that you are taking consistent action towards your goals. Some tips for making positive habits a priority include:

Incorporating positive habits into your daily routine, so that they become a habit

Setting reminders and notifications to help you stay on track

Keeping a journal to track your progress and celebrate your successes

Surrounding yourself with supportive people who will encourage and motivate you

Step 5: Evaluate and Adjust Your Routine

Finally, it is important to evaluate and adjust your daily routine on a regular basis. This involves reflecting on your progress and making any necessary changes to your schedule or habits. Some questions to consider when evaluating your daily routine include:

Are you making consistent progress towards your goals?

Are your positive habits becoming habits?

Are there any obstacles or distractions that are hindering your progress?

By building a daily routine for positive habits, you are taking control of your life and building a foundation for success. This process helps you to prioritize positive habits, take consistent action towards your goals, and achieve success and happiness in all areas of your life.

Of course, establishing a daily routine of positive habits is a crucial step in creating a successful life. This process allows you to prioritize your positive habits, take consistent action towards your goals, and ultimately achieve success and fulfillment in all aspects of your life. By incorporating positive habits into your daily routine, you can set yourself up for success and create a life of joy and abundance.

಄

"You can't build a reputation on what you are
going to do."

- Henry Ford

IV
Overcoming Procrastination and Staying Focused

Procrastination and a lack of focus are two of the biggest obstacles to building positive habits and achieving success. If you find yourself putting off important tasks, or if you struggle to stay focused and on track, then it is essential that you take steps to overcome these obstacles and build the habits and routines that will help you to achieve your goals.

In this chapter, we will explore the causes of procrastination and a lack of focus, and the strategies that you can use to overcome these obstacles and build a productive and successful life.

What Causes Procrastination and a Lack of Focus?

Procrastination and a lack of focus can be caused by a variety of factors, including:

Fear of failure or success

Perfectionism and a need for everything to be just right

Feeling overwhelmed or stressed

A lack of motivation or direction

Boredom or a lack of interest in the task at hand

Distractions and interruptions

Strategies for Overcoming Procrastination and Staying Focused

The following are some strategies that you can use to overcome procrastination and stay focused:

Prioritize your tasks:

Make a list of your most important tasks, and focus on completing these first. By prioritizing your tasks, you will ensure that you are making progress towards your goals and avoiding procrastination.

Set specific and achievable goals:

Make sure that your goals are specific and achievable, and

break them down into smaller, more manageable tasks. This will help you to stay focused and avoid feeling overwhelmed.

Eliminate distractions:

Identify the distractions that are hindering your focus, and take steps to eliminate or minimize them. This might include turning off your phone, closing your email, or finding a quiet place to work.

Stay motivated:

Find ways to stay motivated and focused, such as setting rewards for completing tasks, working with a partner, or tracking your progress.

Use positive self-talk:

Encourage yourself and stay positive, even when faced with setbacks or obstacles. Remind yourself of the reasons why you started, and how far you have come.

Take breaks:

Taking breaks is important for staying focused and avoiding burnout. Make sure to take breaks throughout the day, and engage in activities that refresh and recharge you.

Practice self-care:

Make time for self-care and engage in activities that promote your mental and physical health. This will help you to stay focused, motivated, and productive.

By using these strategies to overcome procrastination and stay focused, you will be able to build the habits and routines that will help you to achieve your goals and build a successful life.

Surely, overcoming procrastination and staying focused are key to building positive habits and achieving success. By using the strategies outlined in this chapter, you can overcome these obstacles and build a productive and successful life. Remember to prioritize your tasks, set achievable goals, eliminate distractions, stay motivated, use positive self-talk, take breaks, and practice self-care. By doing so, you will be on your way to building a foundation of positive habits and achieving the success and happiness that you desire.

"Successful people are not gifted; they just
work hard, then succeed on purpose."

- G.K. Nielson

೮౩

V
Building Mental and Physical Resilience

Resilience is the ability to bounce back from adversity and overcome challenges. It is an essential component of success, and a key ingredient in building positive habits and achieving your goals. In order to be resilient, you need to have a strong foundation of mental and physical health.

In this chapter, we will explore the importance of building mental and physical resilience, and the strategies that you can use to strengthen your resilience and build a strong foundation for success.

The Importance of Mental and Physical Resilience

Mental and physical resilience are critical for success, as they help you to:

Overcome adversity: Resilience helps you to bounce back from setbacks, failures, and obstacles, and to keep pushing forward towards your goals.

Stay focused: Resilience helps you to stay focused and motivated, even in the face of challenges and distractions.

Maintain a positive outlook: Resilience helps you to maintain a positive outlook and to stay optimistic, even in the face of adversity.

Manage stress: Resilience helps you to manage stress and to avoid burnout, allowing you to stay focused and productive.

Strategies for Building Mental and Physical Resilience

The following are some strategies that you can use to build mental and physical resilience:

Exercise regularly: Exercise is one of the best ways to build mental and physical resilience. It releases endorphins, reduces stress, and improves overall physical and mental health.

Get enough sleep: Sleep is essential for mental and physical health, and helps to recharge your batteries and boost your resilience.

Eat a healthy diet: A healthy diet provides the nutrients that your body needs to function at its best, and helps to reduce stress and promote mental and physical health.

Practice mindfulness: Mindfulness helps to calm the mind, reduce stress, and improve focus and resilience.

Surround yourself with positive people: Surrounding yourself with positive and supportive people will help you to maintain a positive outlook, reduce stress, and build resilience.

Focus on the present moment: Focusing on the present moment and practicing gratitude helps to reduce stress, maintain a positive outlook, and build resilience.

Set achievable goals: Setting achievable goals and breaking them down into smaller, more manageable tasks helps to reduce stress and build resilience.

Practice self-care: Taking care of yourself is essential for building resilience, and can include activities such as meditation, yoga, or simply taking a relaxing bath.

By using these strategies to build mental and physical resilience, you will be able to strengthen your foundation for success, and to overcome adversity and achieve your goals.

Yes, building mental and physical resilience is essential for success. By using the strategies outlined in this chapter, you can build a strong foundation for success and overcome adversity, even in the face of challenges and distractions. Remember to exercise regularly, get enough sleep, eat a healthy diet, practice mindfulness, surround yourself with positive people, focus on the present moment, set achievable goals, and practice self-care. By doing so, you will be well on your way to building a life of positive habits and achieving the success and happiness that you desire.

"Your positive action combined with positive
thinking results in success."

- Shiv Khera

VI

Understanding and Managing Negative Emotions

Negative emotions such as anger, frustration, sadness, and anxiety can be overwhelming and can get in the way of our success. These emotions can cause us to engage in unhealthy behaviors and can sabotage our positive habits. Understanding and managing these negative emotions is critical for building a foundation of positive habits and achieving success.

The Nature of Negative Emotions

Negative emotions are a natural and normal part of life. They serve as a response to stressful or challenging situations and help us to navigate difficult circumstances. However, when negative emotions become intense and persistent, they can interfere with our daily lives and impact our well-being.

Strategies for Managing Negative Emotions

The following are some strategies that you can use to manage and overcome negative emotions:

Identify the cause: *Understanding the cause of your negative emotions can help you to address and manage them more effectively.*

Practice self-reflection: *Reflecting on your thoughts and emotions can help you to understand and manage them more effectively.*

Engage in physical activity: *Exercise is a powerful tool for managing negative emotions, as it releases endorphins and helps to reduce stress and anxiety.*

Use positive self-talk: *Using positive self-talk can help to reframe negative thoughts and to reduce the impact of negative emotions.*

Practice mindfulness: *Mindfulness can help to calm the mind and reduce negative emotions, by focusing on the present moment and reducing worry and anxiety.*

Connect with others: *Connecting with others can help to reduce feelings of isolation and to build resilience and positive emotions.*

Seek support: *Seeking support from a trusted friend, family member, or mental health professional can be an effective way* *to manage negative emotions and to build resilience.*

Focus on the positive: *Focusing on the positive aspects of life and practicing gratitude can help to reduce negative emotions and to build resilience.*

By using these strategies to manage negative emotions, you will be able to overcome the obstacles that they present and to build a foundation of positive habits and success.

Surely, negative emotions are a normal part of life, but they can interfere with our well-being and success. By using the strategies outlined in this chapter, you can effectively manage and overcome these emotions, and build a foundation of positive habits and success. Remember to identify the cause of your negative emotions, practice self-reflection, engage in physical activity, use positive self-talk, practice mindfulness, connect with others, seek support, and focus on the positive. By doing so, you will be well on your way to achieving the success and happiness that you desire.

"*Success is the result of small daily actions repeated consistently over time.*"

- John C. Maxwell

ॐ

VII
Building Self-Esteem through Positive Affirmations

Self-esteem is a crucial component of personal well-being and success. It refers to our overall sense of self-worth and can influence the way we view ourselves, our relationships, and the world around us. Positive affirmations are statements or phrases that are used to reinforce positive beliefs and values, and can be an effective tool for building self-esteem.

The Importance of Self-Esteem

Self-esteem is an essential aspect of personal well-being, as it influences the way we perceive ourselves and the world around us. People with high self-esteem generally feel confident, optimistic, and secure in their abilities and relationships. On the other hand, individuals with low self-esteem may struggle with feelings of insecurity, self-doubt, and anxiety.

Low self-esteem can also have a significant impact on our personal and professional lives. For example, individuals with low self-esteem may avoid taking risks, engaging in new activities, or pursuing their goals. They may also struggle to form healthy relationships, as they may believe that they are unworthy of love and affection.

The Power of Positive Affirmations

Positive affirmations are statements or phrases that are used to reinforce positive beliefs and values. They are designed to counteract negative thoughts and emotions, and to promote self-confidence and self-esteem. By repeating positive affirmations regularly, you can replace negative beliefs with positive ones, and cultivate a more positive outlook on life.

Positive affirmations can be used in a variety of ways, including writing them down, repeating them out loud, or visualizing them. The following are some examples of positive affirmations that you can use to build self-esteem:

"I am capable and deserving of success."

"I am confident in my abilities and decisions."

"I am worthy of love and respect."

"I trust in my own journey and path in life."

"I am strong and resilient."

Using positive affirmations regularly can help to improve self-esteem, increase self-confidence, and enhance overall well-being. Furthermore, incorporating positive affirmations into your daily routine can help to make them a habit, allowing you to reap their benefits over the long-term.

Self-esteem is a crucial aspect of personal well-being and success. Positive affirmations can be an effective tool for building self-esteem and countering negative thoughts and emotions. By using positive affirmations regularly, you can replace negative beliefs with positive ones, and cultivate a more positive outlook on life. Remember to use positive affirmations in a variety of ways, such as writing them down, repeating them out loud, or visualizing them. With time and practice, positive affirmations can become a positive habit, helping you to build self-esteem, increase self-confidence, and enhance your overall well-being.

"The greatest glory in living lies not in never falling, but in rising every time we fall."

- Nelson Mandela

ଓଃ

VIII

The Power of Positive Thinking and Gratitude

Positive thinking and gratitude are two powerful habits that can significantly impact our personal and professional lives. These habits can help to improve our mental and emotional well-being, and lead to greater success and happiness. In this chapter, we will explore the benefits of positive thinking and gratitude, and how they can be incorporated into our daily lives.

The Benefits of Positive Thinking

Positive thinking is the practice of focusing on the good in every situation, and approaching life with an optimistic and hopeful outlook. This habit can have numerous benefits, including:

Improved mental health: Positive thinking can help to reduce stress and anxiety, and increase feelings of happiness and well-being.

Better relationships: Positive thinking can lead to better communication and relationships with others, as individuals with a positive outlook are generally more likable and approachable.

Increased resilience: Positive thinking can help individuals to bounce back from setbacks and challenges more quickly, and to view difficulties as opportunities for growth and learning.

Improved physical health: Positive thinking has been linked to improved physical health, as it can reduce stress, which has been linked to numerous physical health problems.

The Benefits of Gratitude

Gratitude is the practice of focusing on what we have, rather than what we lack. This habit can have numerous benefits, including:

Increased happiness: Gratitude has been linked to increased feelings of happiness, as it helps individuals to focus on the good in their lives, rather than dwelling on the negative.

Improved relationships: Gratitude can lead to better relationships with others, as individuals who practice gratitude tend to be more appreciative and less critical of others.

Better physical health: Gratitude has been linked to improved physical health, as it can reduce stress and anxiety, and improve sleep.

Increased resilience: Gratitude can help individuals to bounce back from setbacks and challenges more quickly, and to view difficulties as opportunities for growth and learning.

Incorporating Positive Thinking and Gratitude into Daily Life

Positive thinking and gratitude can be incorporated into daily life in a variety of ways, including:

Keeping a gratitude journal: Writing down what you are grateful for each day can help to cultivate a habit of gratitude.

Practicing affirmations: Repeating positive affirmations each day can help to replace negative thoughts with positive ones, and cultivate a habit of positive thinking.

Spending time with positive people: Surrounding yourself with positive and optimistic individuals can help to improve your outlook on life.

Engaging in acts of kindness: Performing acts of kindness, such as volunteering, can help to increase feelings of happiness and gratitude.

Practicing mindfulness: Engaging in mindfulness activities, such as meditation, can help to reduce stress and increase feelings of gratitude.

Yes, positive thinking and gratitude are two powerful habits that can significantly impact our personal and professional lives. These habits can help to improve mental and emotional well-being, and lead to greater success and happiness. By incorporating positive thinking and gratitude into daily life, individuals can cultivate these habits and reap their benefits over the long-term. Whether through keeping a gratitude journal, practicing affirmations, spending time with positive people, engaging in acts of kindness, or practicing mindfulness, there are numerous ways to incorporate positive thinking and gratitude into daily life. By doing so, individuals can build a foundation of success, and live a life filled with happiness, well-being, and fulfillment.

"Success is the sum of small efforts repeated
day in and day out."

- Robert Collier

∞

IX

Dealing with Failure and Learning from Mistakes

One of the biggest obstacles in the journey towards success is the fear of failure. Unfortunately, failure is inevitable and is a part of the learning process. However, the way we deal with failure can either hold us back or propel us forward. The key is to have a positive attitude towards failure and use it as an opportunity to learn and grow.

In order to develop a positive attitude towards failure, it's important to understand that failure is not a reflection of your worth as a person. It's simply a result of not achieving a specific goal. Instead of seeing failure as a personal defeat, reframe it as a valuable lesson that can help you grow and improve.

It's also important to understand that failure is not permanent. You can always pick yourself up, dust yourself off and try again. Successful people understand that failure is just a temporary setback and that success is a journey with ups and downs.

One of the most important steps in dealing with failure is to take responsibility for your actions. It's important to avoid blaming others or making excuses. Instead, take the time to reflect on what went wrong and what you can do differently next time. This will help you gain valuable insights and improve your chances of success in the future.

Another important aspect of dealing with failure is to maintain a positive attitude and focus on the things that you can control. Instead of dwelling on the past, focus on what you can do in the present to move forward. Cultivate a growth mindset by focusing on your strengths and working to improve your weaknesses.

Finally, it's important to celebrate your successes, no matter how small they may be. Celebrating your successes, even the small ones, will help you maintain a positive attitude and stay motivated in the face of failure.

Surely, dealing with failure is a critical component of success. It's important to develop a positive attitude towards failure and use it as an opportunity to learn and grow. By taking responsibility for your actions, focusing on the things you can control, and celebrating your successes, you will be well on your way to building a foundation of success.

"*Successful and unsuccessful people do not vary greatly in their abilities. They vary in their desires to reach their potential.*"

- John Maxwell

X

Building a Support System and Connecting with Others

Building a support system and connecting with others is a crucial component of success. Having a supportive network of friends, family, and mentors can help you stay motivated, overcome challenges, and achieve your goals.

First and foremost, it's important to surround yourself with positive and supportive people who believe in you and your goals. Surrounding yourself with people who are positive and encouraging will help you maintain a positive attitude and keep you motivated.

Another important aspect of building a support system is to seek out mentors and role models who can provide guidance and support. Having a mentor or role model can help you stay on track, learn from others who have already achieved success, and get valuable feedback and advice.

It's also important to participate in activities and engage in hobbies that you enjoy. Joining a group or club that aligns with your interests can help you connect with like-minded people, develop new skills, and provide a sense of community.

Another way to build a support system is to volunteer and give back to others. Volunteering provides an opportunity to connect with others and make a difference in your community. It also helps you develop a sense of purpose and feel good about yourself.

Finally, it's important to prioritize self-care and make time for yourself. Taking care of yourself, both physically and mentally, is essential to maintaining a positive attitude and staying motivated. Engaging in activities that bring you joy, such as reading, exercising, or meditating, can help you reduce stress and improve your overall well-being.

Building a support system and connecting with others is a critical component of success. Surrounding yourself with positive and supportive people, seeking out mentors and role models, participating in activities and hobbies you enjoy, volunteering, and prioritizing self-care are all important steps in building a foundation of success. By taking these steps, you will be well on your way to achieving your goals and living a happy and fulfilling life.

☙

"*Success is doing what you love, and doing it well.*"

- Maya Angelou

ॐ

XI

Finding and Pursuing Your Passions

Finding and pursuing your passions is an important step towards building a fulfilling and successful life. When you're passionate about something, you're more likely to be motivated and dedicated to making progress, and you're more likely to enjoy the journey along the way.

So, how do you find your passions? It can be helpful to start by reflecting on your interests, values, and strengths. What are you naturally drawn to? What activities do you enjoy doing in your free time? What values and beliefs are most important to you? What are you good at and what do others compliment you on? These are all clues that can help you identify your passions.

It's also helpful to try new things and explore different

interests. Take a class in a subject that interests you, join a club or organization, or volunteer in a new area. You never know what you may discover that ignites a passion within you.

Once you've identified your passions, it's time to pursue them. Start small by incorporating your passions into your daily routine. Maybe it's reading for 20 minutes a day about a topic that interests you or taking a class in the evenings. Then, gradually increase the time and effort you invest in pursuing your passions.

It's also important to be patient and persistent. Pursuing your passions is a journey, not a destination. There will be setbacks and challenges along the way, but it's important to stay focused and dedicated to your goals.

One of the keys to pursuing your passions is to set achievable goals and develop a plan to reach those goals. This could mean setting short-term and long-term goals, breaking down larger goals into smaller, manageable tasks, and regularly reviewing your progress. Having a clear plan and a roadmap to follow can help you stay motivated and on track.

Finally, it's important to surround yourself with supportive people who encourage and believe in you. Seek out mentors, join a community of people who share your interests, and connect with others who can provide support and encouragement along the way.

Yes, finding and pursuing your passions is an important step towards building a fulfilling and successful life. Take the time to reflect on your interests, values, and strengths, explore new activities and interests, set achievable goals, and surround yourself with supportive people. By doing so, you'll be well on your way to living a life filled with passion and purpose.

*"Success is not just about what you achieve,
but about what you overcome."*

- Oprah Winfrey

൫

XII

Understanding and Managing Perfectionism

Perfectionism can be a double-edged sword. On one hand, it can drive you to strive for excellence and push you to achieve your goals. On the other hand, it can be a major obstacle to success, causing you to be overly critical of yourself, fear taking risks, and struggle to complete tasks.

Perfectionism can be defined as a relentless pursuit of excellence or an unrelenting need for flawlessness. It's the belief that anything less than perfect is unacceptable and that you must meet impossibly high standards to be successful. Perfectionism can lead to stress, anxiety, and low self-esteem, making it difficult to achieve your goals and live a fulfilling life.

The good news is that perfectionism can be managed. Here are some strategies for managing perfectionism:

Set realistic and achievable goals. Perfectionists often set unrealistic goals for themselves, which can be stressful and demotivating. Instead, set achievable goals that are challenging but realistic, and focus on making progress rather than being perfect.

Practice self-compassion. Perfectionists are often overly critical of themselves, but self-compassion can help you be kinder and more understanding of yourself. When you make a mistake or fall short of your goals, focus on what you can learn from the experience and how you can improve, rather than berating yourself.

Focus on progress, not perfection. Instead of striving for perfection, focus on making progress and celebrating your successes, no matter how small. Celebrate your accomplishments and take pride in what you've achieved, even if it's not perfect.

Learn to say no. Perfectionists often feel the need to take on too many tasks and responsibilities, leading to burnout and stress. It's important to learn to say no to tasks that are not a priority or that you don't have the time or energy for.

Embrace imperfection. Perfectionism often leads to procrastination and fear of taking risks. Embrace imperfection and take the pressure off yourself to be perfect. Instead, focus on making progress, learning from your mistakes, and enjoying the journey.

Perfectionism can be a major obstacle to success, but it can be managed. By setting realistic and achievable goals, practicing self-compassion, focusing on progress, learning to say no, and embracing imperfection, you can overcome perfectionism and build a more fulfilling and successful life.

"*Success is the ability to go from one failure to another with no loss of enthusiasm.*"

- Winston Churchill

ॐ

XIII

Building Self-Compassion

Self-compassion is an essential ingredient in a happy and successful life. It involves treating yourself with kindness, understanding, and care, especially during difficult times. When you practice self-compassion, you cultivate a positive and supportive inner voice, which can provide comfort and motivation during challenging moments.

Self-compassion is often misunderstood as being selfish or indulgent. However, this could not be further from the truth. In reality, self-compassion involves acknowledging and accepting your own shortcomings, mistakes, and imperfections, while also striving to do your best. This perspective can foster resilience, motivation, and a positive attitude, helping you to overcome obstacles and achieve your goals.

There are several benefits to developing self-compassion.

Research has shown that self-compassionate individuals have lower levels of anxiety and depression, higher levels of well-being, and better coping skills. Self-compassion also helps to boost self-esteem and confidence, as well as fostering healthy relationships with others.

There are several ways to build self-compassion in your life. One effective method is through mindfulness meditation. This involves focusing your attention on the present moment and accepting your thoughts and feelings without judgment. Mindfulness meditation can help to increase self-awareness and reduce negative self-talk, leading to greater self-compassion.

Another way to build self-compassion is through positive self-talk. This involves speaking to yourself in a supportive and encouraging manner, just as you would to a friend. It is important to avoid negative self-talk and criticism, and instead focus on what you are doing well and what you are grateful for.

Another effective way to cultivate self-compassion is through journaling. This involves writing down your thoughts, feelings, and experiences, and reflecting on them in a non-judgmental way. Journaling can help to process difficult emotions and develop a more compassionate perspective towards yourself.

Finally, self-compassion can be enhanced through acts of kindness towards yourself. This involves treating yourself with care and respect, such as taking time for self-care, practicing gratitude, and setting healthy boundaries.

Self-compassion is a powerful tool for building a foundation of success in your life. By treating yourself with kindness, understanding, and care, you can foster resilience, motivation, and a positive attitude, helping you to overcome obstacles and achieve your goals. Remember to be patient with yourself, as building self-compassion is a journey, not a destination.

*"Success is stumbling from failure to failure
with no loss of enthusiasm."*

- Abraham Lincoln

XIV

The Role of Mindfulness in Positive Habits

Mindfulness is a mental state achieved by focusing one's awareness on the present moment, while calmly acknowledging and accepting one's feelings, thoughts, and bodily sensations. It has become a popular tool in promoting well-being and personal growth and is now widely used in various fields, including psychology, healthcare, and education.

Incorporating mindfulness into your daily routine can play a significant role in building positive habits and promoting success. Here's how:

Improved self-awareness: Mindfulness helps you develop a better understanding of yourself and your emotions. This self-awareness can be a powerful tool in building positive habits, as you'll be more aware of your triggers and patterns of behavior that may be hindering your success. By taking time to reflect on your thoughts and feelings, you can gain insight into what drives your behavior, and make changes to help you stay on track towards your goals.

Reduced stress and anxiety: Mindfulness can help to reduce stress and anxiety levels, which can be a major hindrance to your success. When you're in a state of mindfulness, you're able to take a step back from the demands of life and see things from a different perspective. This can help you to feel less overwhelmed, allowing you to make clearer decisions and take action towards your goals with less stress and anxiety.

Increased focus and productivity: Mindfulness helps to improve concentration and focus, which is essential for success in any area of life. When you're in a state of mindfulness, you're able to prioritize your thoughts and eliminate distractions. This allows you to be more productive, as you'll be better able to stay focused on the task at hand and complete it more efficiently.

Improved relationships: Mindfulness also plays a crucial role in building positive relationships. By developing greater self-awareness and empathy, you can better understand the needs of others and respond to them in a more positive and constructive way. This can lead to improved communication, more meaningful connections, and greater success in personal and professional relationships.

So, how can you incorporate mindfulness into your daily

routine? Here are some practical tips:

Start small: Incorporating mindfulness into your daily routine doesn't need to be complicated or time-consuming. Start by taking just a few minutes each day to focus on your breath and bring your attention to the present moment. Over time, you can increase the amount of time you spend in mindfulness as you see the benefits it brings.

Practice regularly: The key to incorporating mindfulness into your daily routine is to make it a regular habit. Try to make time for mindfulness at the same time each day, so that it becomes a routine that you can look forward to.

Use mindfulness apps: There are many mindfulness apps available that can help you develop a regular mindfulness practice. These apps can provide guidance and support to help you build mindfulness into your daily routine, and make it easier to stick to.

Incorporate mindfulness into other activities: Mindfulness can be integrated into many aspects of your life, such as your work, exercise routine, or daily commute. For example, you could try practicing mindfulness while walking, cooking, or doing yoga.

Mindfulness is a powerful tool in building positive habits and promoting success. By incorporating mindfulness into your daily routine, you can improve your self-awareness, reduce stress and anxiety, increase focus and productivity, and improve your relationships. So, why not give it a try today, and start building the foundation for a successful, mindful life!

"Success is not how high you have climbed,
but how you make a positive difference to the
world."

- Roy T. Bennett

ॐ

XV

Building Your Life on a Foundation of Success Through Positive Habits

Congratulations on reaching the end of this journey towards building a life on a foundation of success through positive habits. This book has provided you with the knowledge, tools, and strategies to develop and maintain positive habits that will help you achieve your goals, boost your self-esteem, and increase your overall well-being. Throughout the book, you have learned about the importance of setting goals, building a daily routine, overcoming procrastination, building mental and physical resilience, managing negative emotions, and cultivating positive thinking, gratitude, self-compassion, and mindfulness. You have also learned about the importance of connecting with others, finding and pursuing your passions, and dealing with failure and learning from mistakes.

To recap, positive habits have a profound impact on our lives. By consistently practicing positive habits, we can develop a positive mindset, increase our motivation and focus, and build resilience to handle life's challenges. Positive habits can help us improve our relationships, foster personal growth, and lead a life filled with meaning and purpose.

So, what now? The final step is to put all of these habits into practice and create a daily routine that works for you. Start with small, manageable habits and focus on one habit at a time. As you become more comfortable and confident, you can add more habits to your routine. Remember to be patient and compassionate with yourself, and don't be discouraged if it takes time to establish new habits. Celebrate your successes, no matter how small, and be kind to yourself when you stumble. The journey towards a successful and fulfilling life through positive habits is a lifelong one, but by taking small steps each day, you will eventually reach your destination.

In conclusion, the power of positive habits lies in their ability to transform our lives for the better. By consistently practicing positive habits, we can build a foundation of success that will help us achieve our goals, improve our relationships, and lead a life filled with meaning and purpose. Remember to be kind to yourself, celebrate your successes, and keep pushing forward, no matter how small the steps. You have the power to build the life you want, and with the right habits, you can achieve anything you set your mind to.

ॐ

"Success is not final, failure is not fatal: it's
the courage to continue that counts."

- John Wooden.

೮೪

OTHER BOOKS OF THE AUTHOR

1. The Moments When I Met God
2. Kashiyile Theertha Pathangal
3. Guru Gyan Vani
4. Abhiprerak Gita
5. Assi Se Jain Ghat Tak
6. Hopelessness Of Arjuna
7. The Soul And It's True Nature
8. Sense Of Action (Karma)
9. Action Through Wisdom
10. Action Through Wisdom
11. Theory And Practical Of Every Action
12. Logical Understanding Of The Supreme
13. The Imperishable Supreme
14. Yatra Nishadraj Se Hanuman Ghat Tak
15. Yatra Karnatak Ghat Se Raja Ghat Tak
16. Yatra Pandey Ghat Se Prayagraj Ghat Tak
17. Yatra Ranjendra Prasad Ghat Se Dattatreya Ghat Tak
18. Yaatrasindhiya Ghat Se Gwaliar Ghat Tak
19. Yatra Mangala Gauri Ghat Se Hanuman Gadhi Ghat Tak
20. Yatra Gaay Ghat Se Nishad Ghat Tak
21. Maa Ganga, Ghaten Evm Utsav
22. Ganga Arti Dev Deepavali Evam Any Utsav
23. Potentials Of Digitalized India
24. Vedic Consciousness
25. A Brief Introduction To Vedic Science
26. Kashi Ke Barah Jyotirling
27. Impact Of Motivation
28. Let's Have A Milky Way Journey
29. Color Therapy In A Nutshell

30. Rigveda In A Nutshell
31. Yajurveda In A Nutshell
32. Samveda In A Nutshell
33. Atharva Veda In A Nutshell
34. Ayushman Bhava - Ayurveda
35. Srimad Bhagavad Gita And Upanishad Connection
36. Srimad Bhagavad Gita - An Attempt To Summarize Each Chapter.
37. Facts And Impact Of Nakshatra
38. Astro Gems - Navaratna
39. Ekadashi - A Concise Overview
40. A Concise View Of Hanuman Chalisa
41. Inspirational Gita
42. Nakshatraranyam
43. Summary Of 18 Mahapuranas
44. Synopsis Of 18 Upa Puranas
45. Rigvediya Upanishads
46. Shukla Yajurvediya Upanishads
47. Krishna Yajurvediya Upanishads
48. Samavediya Upanishads
49. Atharvavediya Upanishads
50. The Seven Great Sages
51. From Rocket Scientist To President Dr. Apj Abdul Kalam
52. The Visionary's Voice - Quotes Of Dr. Apj Abdul Kalam
53. The Wisdom Of Swami Vivekananda: Insights And Inspiration From A Legendary Spiritual Teacher
54. Ayurvedic Remedies From The Garden
55. Sages And Seers
56. Rising Strong – Motivational Stories Of Women
57. Beyond Flames -Mystery Stories Of Funeral Ghat Manikarnika
58. The Origins Of Tulsi: A Look At The Mythological Roots Of The Plant"

59. The Holistic Cow: A Look At The Physical, Spiritual, And Cultural Importance Of Cows In India
60. Arts Of Healing
61. Exploring The Divine
62. Understanding Five Elements
63. The Etymology Of Ram
64. Symbols Of India
65. Voice Of Change (About Speeches Of Great Men)
66. She Speaks (About Speeches Of Great Women)
67. Patriotism On Celluloid – Brief About Patriotic Films
68. The Music Of Motivation: A Brief Guide To Inspirational Film Songs
69. **Unlocking The Secrets of The Dashopanishads**
70. A Cultural Mosaic
71. Ancient Traditions, Modern Minds
72. Ecos Of Ancient Wisdom
73. Beneath The Surface
74. From Temples To Ashrams
75. Sages Of The Subcontinent
76. The Art Of Healling (Ayurveda, Yoga & Naturopathy)
77. Indian Kitchen
78. The Festivals Of India
79. The Indian Epics Retold
80. The Power Of Mantras
81. The Indian River Ganges
82. The Indian Architecture
83. Rites Of Passage
84. The Indian Silk Road
85. The Indian Literature
86. The Indian Villages
87. The Indian Folks & Crafts
88. The Way Of Buddha
89. The Ramayan Of Tulsidas

90. Astrological Remedies
91. The Secret Power Of Motivation
92. Secret Of Developing Your Inner Strength
93. The Secret Path To Motivation
94. The Art And Secret Of Positive Thinking
95. The Secrets Of Practicing Ethical Living
96. Indian Art And Painting
97. The Indian Herbalism
98. Bharatanatyam To Kathak
99. Exploring India's Astrological Remedies
100. The Indian Festival Of Flowers
101. Indian Handicrafts
102. The Splashes Of Joy – India's Colour Festival
103. The Indian Science Of Astrology
104. The Indian Mythology
105. Path To Enlightenment
106. The Indian Spirituality For Children
107. Aromas Of India
108. The Secrets Of Healthy Relationships
109. Ancestral Ties
110. The Indian Street Food
111. Discovering America
112. The Indian Textile
113. Listening To Motivational Speeches
114. Taste Of India
115. A Cultural Journey Through Indian Nuptials
116. Motivational Quote For Change
117. Secret Strategies For Making Money
118. Secrets To Cultivate A Positive Mindset
119. A Tapestry Of Cultures: Exploring India From Kashmir To Kanyakumari
120. Achieving Your Dreams With Resilience: Secret Strategies For Overcoming Obstacles

121. Innovative Startups - 25 Startup Ideas To Spark Your Business Creativity
122. Export Management: Strategies For Global Success
123. Exporting From India - A Step By Step Guide
124. Finance Fundamentals: Mastering Financial Management For Business Success
125. Global Growth Strategies For International Business Development
126. Marketing Mastery: Unlocking The Secrets Of Modern Marketing
127. Operations Mastery: Managing The Flow Of Value In Business
128. Strategic Business Management: Navigating The Modern Business Landscape
129. Human Resource Management Strategies For Building And Managing A High Performance Team
130. The Indian Landscapes And Nature: An Exploration Of India's Natural Beauty And Diversity
131. The Indian Street Performances: A Cultural Exploration Of India's Street Performances
132. Affirming Your Self-Worth: Strategies For Achieving Emotional Wellbeing
133. Cultivating Self-Discipline: Secrets Methods For Achieving Your Goals
134. Embracing Change: Strategies For Adapting To Life's Challenges
135. Embracing Your Uniqueness: Secret Strategies For Living An Authentic Life
136. Finding Motivation In Despondency: Coping With Difficult Times
137. Embracing Change
138. Learning To Love Yourself
139. Managing Time For Yourself

140. Unlock The Keys To Self-Motivation
141. Secret To Boost Confidence
142. Unlocking Your Potential: A Path To Inner-Strength & Success
143. Secrets To Develop Authentic Relationship
144. Secrets To Build A Successful Career
145. Secrets To Live With Gratitude
146. Secrets To Create A Life Of Abundance
147. Secrets To Cultivate Self-Awareness
148. The Power Of Helping Hands
149. Finding Your Passion
150. The Indian Mythical Creatures
151. The Indian Women Saints
152. The Wisdom Of The Saints
153. "The Indian Royalty: A Cultural And Historical Exploration Of India's Maharajas And Their Kingdom"
154. The Mystic Land: A Cultural And Spiritual Exploration Of India"
155. India's Spiritual Legacy – Discovering The Cultural And Religious Significance Of Bhakti Yoga.
156. The Indian Folktales: An Exploration Of India's Oral Folklore Traditions
157. Steeping In History: A Look At India's Iconic Tea Culture
158. The Indian Way Of Life: An Exploration Of The Philosophy And Practices Of Indian Culture
159. From Silence To Sound: A Cultural And Historical Study Of Indian Cinema
160. Chronicles Of Indian Style: Tracing The Transformations Of Traditional And Contemporary Fashion
161. Decorating India: A Journey Through The Traditions And Transformations Of Home Design
162. Adornments Of India: A Journey Through The History

Contact

DR. JAGADEESH PILLAI

MBA & PhD in Vedic Science

Four Times Guinness World Record Holder

Winner of Mahatma Gandhi Vishwa Shanti Puraskar and
Global Peace Ambassador

Gemology, Astro & Vastu Consultant - Spiritual Counselor

Consultant for designing World Record Ideas

Efficient Tarot Card Reader

9839093003

myrichindia@gmail.com

drjagadeeshpillai@facebook

drjagadeeshpillai@instagram
jagadeeshpillai@youtube

www. JAGADEESHPILLAI.com